Steck-Vaughn

Think-Alongs™

Comprehending As You Read

Level E

Program Authors

Senior Author
Roger Farr

Co-Authors
Jennifer Conner
Elizabeth Haydel
Bruce Tone
Beth Greene
Tanja Bisesi
Cheryl Gilliland

STECK-VAUGHN
C O M P A N Y

A Division of Harcourt Brace & Company

www.steck-vaughn.com

Acknowledgments

Editorial Director	Diane Schnell
Project Editor	Anne Souby
Associate Director of Design	Cynthia Ellis
Design Manager	Ted Krause
Production and Design	Julia Miracle-Hagaman
Photo Editor	Claudette Landry
Product Manager	Patricia Colacino
Cover Design	Ted Krause
Cover Sculpture	Lonnie Springer
Cover Production	Alan Klemp

Think-Alongs™ is a trademark of Steck-Vaughn Company.

ISBN 0-7398-0087-6

1 2 3 4 5 6 7 8 9 0   PO   03 02 01 00 99

Contents

Drawing Conclusions

Read the selection below. As you read, think about conclusions you can draw.

Daniel turned over the old log in the woods. He saw some insects that looked like pale ants all over it. The bottom of the log looked like it was turning to sawdust. Daniel could see many holes and tunnels in the log. The whitish insects scurried into the tunnels. Daniel ran to the house to get a jar so he could take some to school to show his teacher.

This selection contains information, or clues. By putting together the clues, you can draw conclusions. Check the boxes next to your conclusions.

I think Daniel likes to collect insects.

The clues helped me draw these conclusions:

☐ The insects were eating the wood in the log.

☐ The insects did not like bright light.

☐ Daniel's house is near the woods.

What might you conclude about Daniel from reading the selection?

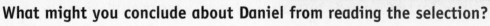

Read and Think

- Read the selections that follow.
- Stop at each box and answer the question.
- Remember to think about drawing conclusions as you read.

Cheetahs Are Fastest

By Jack Myers

Let's Read

This selection is about cheetahs. Read the selection to learn how a scientist concluded that the cheetah is the fastest animal on earth.

How fast can animals run? And which is fastest? There are lots of records but also a lot of arguments, mainly because there are many problems in measuring the speed of a wild animal.

To time humans, we use carefully measured tracks, runners started by the sound of a gun, and stopwatches. We can be almost as careful in timing horse races, since the horses are trained and have riders. But that won't work for wild animals.

1   Why is it difficult to measure the speed of animals?

Of course there are some ways to compare speeds of different animals. A predator like a cheetah can make a living by running fast to catch up to its prey. And its prey includes fast-running animals like gazelles and antelopes. That's where we got the idea that the cheetah may be the fastest running animal. But how can we measure its speed for the record books?

For some animals, speed has been measured by following the animal in a car while watching the speedometer. Others have been timed by filming the animal as it runs, then using the movie to time how long an animal takes to move its own length. Then it takes a measurement of the animal's length and a little math to figure out its speed. Both of those methods leave some room for argument.

 2   How have animals' speeds been measured?

Accurate Measurement

For the cheetah, we now have a measurement of speed done so carefully that it became a scientific experiment. It was done by a British track coach who was visiting in Kenya.

The cheetah in this experiment, Pritchelou, was an orphan that had been brought up on a farm and then returned to the wild. She often came back to the farm, and it was on one of her visits that the measurements were made.

The coach, Mr. N.C.C. Sharp, carefully recorded his experiment. First he measured off a course of 220 yards using a surveyor's tape. That's almost exactly the same length as the 200-meter dash, a distance that sprinters run throughout the world. The track was on level ground and marked by two posts at each end. At the starting end, Mr. Sharp tied a piece of white wool yarn between the posts. At the finish he marked a line on the ground between the two posts. To make sure his stopwatch was correct, he checked it against two stopwatches of the Kenya Athletic Association. Then he picked a quiet, windless day for the experiment.

 3 How can you tell that the experiment was carefully designed?

To get ready for each test, the cheetah was held 18 yards behind the starting line. A truck, with its engine running and ready to go, was 75 yards down the course.

The coach stood in the back of the truck. In one hand he held the stopwatch, in the other a piece of meat that had been shown to the cheetah. He shouted for the cheetah to be released, and started the stopwatch when she broke the yarn at the starting point. A driver revved up the truck to stay ahead of the cheetah until well beyond the finish line. The coach stopped the watch when he saw the chest of the cheetah cross the finish line. Then he threw down the meat to let the cheetah eat it.

4   Why was a piece of meat used?

Two more trials were made, with a thirty-minute rest between them. The times for the three trials were 7.0, 6.9, and 7.2 seconds.

The Cheetah's Time

Mr. Sharp chose the average of 7.0 seconds as the time it took the cheetah to run 220 yards. If you want to do the math, you can figure that the average speed was 31 yards per second, or 29 meters per second, or 65 miles per hour.

For comparison, a racehorse can run about 41 miles per hour, and champion human sprinters run only about 23 miles per hour.

 5 What can you conclude about the speed of a cheetah?

The design of Mr. Sharp's experiment meant that the cheetah purposely was given a running start. That gives the cheetah a little advantage over other animals, such as racehorses, which are timed from a standing start. But the cheetah is so much faster that it leaves no doubt that it is the world's fastest running animal.

Of course, like most scientific experiments, this one was not perfect. It did not answer all the questions you might like to ask. A cheetah now holds the record as the world's fastest animal. But we do not know that the cheetah used in the experiment is the world's fastest cheetah.

Time to Write!

This selection describes a scientific experiment that was designed to measure the speed of a cheetah. You are going to design a scientific experiment to measure the speed of another animal.

- For this activity, you will write a report telling how you are going to conduct your experiment.

Prewriting

First, answer the questions below to help plan your report.

What animal will you use in your experiment? _____

How far will the animal run? _____

How will you measure the running speed? _____

How will you get the animal to run fast? _____

How many times will the experiment be repeated? _____

How much rest time will there be between each trial? _____

What will you be able to conclude from your scientific experiment?

_____

_____

_____

Writing

Now, use another sheet of paper to write your report telling how you are going to conduct your experiment.

Stars in His Eyes

By Jack Rightmyer

Let's Read

This selection is an interview with Dr. Carl Sagan, a famous astronomer. Read the interview to find out how he became interested in planets and stars.

*[Editor's Note: This interview was conducted with Dr. Sagan before his death in 1996. The questions he was asked are indicated by a **Q** (question) and his answers are indicated by an **A** (answer).]*

Dr. Carl Sagan has been a leader in space exploration, even though he has never left the Earth. Before the *Apollo* astronauts took off for the moon, he told them what to expect when they landed. He designed many of the experiments that have been carried to the planets and to outer space by the *Mariner, Viking, Voyager,* and *Galileo* probes. And for years he has been searching for life on other planets.

Dr. Sagan has spent most of his life working to help others feel the excitement of science. He was most successful in his popular television series and book—both titled *Cosmos.* He was an astronomer at Cornell University and director of the Laboratory for Planetary Studies. The author talked with Dr. Carl Sagan about how he became an astronomer.

Q: When did you first become interested in the stars?

A: I grew up in Brooklyn, New York. I knew my neighborhood very well. I spent a lot of time playing in the street. It was a city neighborhood that included houses, lampposts, walls, and bushes. But with an early bedtime in the winter, I could look out my window and see the stars, and the stars were not like anything else in my neighborhood.

Q: At the age of five did you know what the stars were?

A: I didn't know what they were, so I asked my friends and some older children. They looked at me funny, like I had asked them a stupid question. I got answers like "They're lights in the sky, kid."

That wasn't much of an answer. What were they? Were they little electric light bulbs held by black wires you couldn't see?

1   What can you conclude about Carl Sagan's curiosity?

Q: Did you ask your teachers at school?

A: It was actually my mother who said to me, "You have a library card now, and you know how to read. Take the streetcar to the library and get a book on stars." So that's what I did.

I remember feeling very afraid when I stepped up to the big librarian and asked for a book on stars. She didn't hesitate at all. She went to a shelf and got me a book, but it was full of pictures of movie stars. I had to go back and explain that this wasn't the kind of star I had in mind. Finally she brought the right book, and I sat down and found out the answer, which was something really stunning.

I found out that the stars are glowing balls of gas. I also found out that the Sun is a star but really close and that the stars are all suns except really far away. I didn't know any physics or mathematics at that time, but I could imagine how far you'd have to move the Sun away from us till it was only as bright as a star. It was in that library, reading that book, that the scale of the universe opened up to me. There was something beautiful about it.

At that young age, I already knew that I'd be very happy if I could devote my life to finding out more about the stars and the planets that go around them. And it's been my great good fortune to do just that.

2 Why did Carl Sagan become so interested in the stars and the planets?

Q: As a kid you must have enjoyed reading.

A: My parents always encouraged me to read, and books kept my interest going about the stars and planets. Every now and then I would think, "Wouldn't it be fun if I had a friend to talk to about the stars?" But there wasn't one.

At least I had my science fiction books to read. I read the Mars novels by Edgar Rice Burroughs, and I began getting a magazine called *Amazing Science Fiction,* which had stories about the universe that really made me think. I also read the novels of Jules Verne and H.G. Wells.

It was around the age of ten or twelve that I started believing there must be life on other planets.

 3 How did Carl Sagan learn so much about stars and planets?

Q: If there are creatures living on another planet, what do you think they would look like?

A: I can't imagine what they'd look like, and they couldn't imagine what we'd look like. All of life on Earth is the same, except for some external differences in form. Every one of us on Earth, from bacteria to human being, is made up of the same kinds of proteins and the same kinds of nucleic acids. But on another planet, everything is different, and I would expect that the organisms would be totally different from us.

Q: Why do you think most people are so interested in finding life on another planet?

A: I think it's because human beings love to be alive, and we are naturally drawn to other things that are alive. Human beings are curious creatures. We want to know about other living things.

4 Why does Carl Sagan think people are interested in life on other planets?

Q: Do you think we should have a manned mission to Mars?

A: I don't think there's any reason to send people to Mars if our goal is to find out about Mars. Let's send robots instead. They're cheaper. There's no risk of human lives. Robots can go to more dangerous places.

But I think there are reasons for sending people there that are not connected to finding out about Mars. Planning for a manned mission to Mars would force us to improve some of our technology. It would encourage the major technological nations to come together for this project.

Space flight also speaks to something deep within us. A human mission to Mars would provide a sense of adventure. It would help to stimulate a new generation of scientists, and it would make all people feel a little more optimistic about what we can do as a planet.

The robot Sojourner explored Mars in 1997.

5   What are you thinking about now?

Q: What advice would you give a young person who wants to become an astronomer?

A: I'd say, "Study physics. But before you can study physics you have to know mathematics, so study mathematics." I would also encourage them to read a lot, be curious, and ask questions.

Q: For more than fifty years, you've been learning about the stars and planets. You've written many books and given many interviews. Do you ever get tired of talking about the universe?

A: Not really. To me it's like being in love. When you're in love, you want to tell the world. I've been in love with science, so it seems the most natural thing in the world to tell people about it.

6 What can you conclude about Carl Sagan's interest in stars and planets?

Time to Write!

You are going to conduct an interview with someone. You will need to plan your interview, take notes during the interview or tape-record it, and write the results of the interview.

- For this activity, you will write interview questions, interview someone, and write the results.

Prewriting

First, write a list of questions to ask. Think of questions beginning with the words below.

Who? _____

What? _____

_____

When? _____

_____

Where? _____

_____

Why? _____

_____

How? _____

_____

Writing

After you have conducted your interview, use another sheet of paper to write the questions and answers from the interview.

All for the Better: A Story of El Barrio

By Nicholasa Mohr

This selection is a chapter from a book about Evelina Lopez, a Puerto Rican girl living in New York City during the Great Depression. Read the selection to learn how Evelina helps her neighbors.

[Editor's Note: The events of this chapter take place not long after Evelina has moved from Puerto Rico to New York City. She lives in El Barrio, a neighborhood with the largest community of Spanish-speaking people in the city. Evelina is living with her aunt, Tía Vincenta, and uncle, Tío Godreau. A young woman named Miriam rents a room for herself and her baby boy, Jorgito, from the family.]

The Great Depression was hurting *El Barrio*, just as it was hurting the rest of the United States. Many people were out of work and unable to feed their families or themselves. Old clothes were repaired, not replaced. Who had money for a new coat or new gloves?

Empty stomachs and worn clothes made February 1935 seem even colder than usual. The Depression was in its sixth year, and people were struggling just to survive. Even those who had jobs, like Tía Vicenta and Tío Godreau, needed to find extra income to make ends meet.

To help those who were suffering the most, President Franklin Delano Roosevelt established food programs for the needy. Unemployed people and people earning very little money were given forms to fill out for extra food. Completed forms were exchanged for food packages at the distribution centers. The government packages included such basics as canned goods, flour, cereal, powdered milk, peanut butter, and cheese.

But to claim their food, people had to complete and return the government forms. For some this wasn't so easy.

When Miriam lost her job, she refused to fill out the forms and go for her food. "I'm no charity case," said Miriam. "I don't want free handouts. I want to work and earn my food." She was not alone in thinking this way.

"It's too humiliating to go with a piece of paper in one's hand to ask for food . . . like a beggar," said their neighbor Señor Sanchez. "No, I can't—I won't—beg for food. No!"

1 What do you think about Miriam's and Señor Sanchez's refusing to take food?

But Evelina could see that many of these people were hungry. Their children went to school without having eaten breakfast. In the streets she saw people selling apples for pennies. She saw homeless people huddled in doorways. She saw people line up by the hundreds in front of soup kitchens waiting to eat. Yet her neighbors refused available food.

This made no sense to Evelina. Without help, Miriam, Jorgito, and Señor Sanchez might soon be huddled in doorways or on soup kitchen lines, too.

Evelina wanted to do something. Her mother had brought her up with a strong sense of right and wrong. Her mother used to tell her that people who work hard and pay taxes deserve some help from the government when times are difficult. The government should help those in need find jobs. It should, her mother said, make sure everyone can live a decent life.

If her mother was right, why did these people refuse to claim food that they needed and deserved? Evelina was confused, so she spoke to her aunt and uncle.

"People are hungry. They would work if there were jobs, but there aren't any. Now they need food to nourish themselves and their families. They are wrong to refuse."

 2 Why does Evelina conclude that Miriam and Señor Sanchez were wrong to refuse the free food?

"Well," said Tío Godreau sadly, "most of them are too ashamed. They don't understand that it's not their fault. Sometimes I take the forms of one or two of our neighbors with me when I go get our food. As long as I'm there I can bring back a few items for them."

"Evelina," Tía Vicenta told her, "we Puerto Ricans are a proud people. We don't want to appear like beggars or charity cases. That's just the way we are. It's our nature. What can we do?"

"No!" answered Evelina. "That food belongs to the people and they should have it. Things must change."

"And who is going to change things, young lady?" asked Tío Godreau.

"I am," said Evelina, smiling. "And you, Tío, are going to help!"

Evelina also spoke to Miriam. "I know how you feel about going for food. But you always talk about how much I help you with Jorgito. Now you must help me. Please come to the distribution center with me and Tío. Help us get the food. Remember, there are many hungry people out there."

Miriam thought about it. "Since I can see how determined you are to do this," said Miriam, "I'll go with you and Godreau."

That week Evelina went to visit as many of her neighbors as she could find who were entitled to food. "Fill out your forms," she told them. "I will get your food for you. Don't worry."

Some still weren't sure. "What if they won't give it to you?" asked Doña Josefina, who lived in a building across the street.

"Then you will be no worse off than you are now," answered Evelina. "But if it works, you will have food on your table."

"Suppose they expect us to come in next time?" another neighbor argued.

"I promise," answered Evelina, "I will go again and again and again." She was determined to help her neighbors. "Just fill out your forms and leave the rest to me."

3 What can you conclude about the kind of person Evelina is?

Once Evelina had convinced her neighbors to give her their completed forms, she faced another big problem. The distribution center was located across town and several stops uptown as well. This meant at least a forty-minute trolley ride. How could she transport food for a dozen families such a long way with only Miriam and her uncle to help her?

"What about your Cousin Santos?" suggested Tía Vicenta. "Maybe he can help. He drives the trolley car that goes by the food center, and it stops right nearby on the corner of 116th Street."

Evelina spoke to Santos. Her cousin agreed to let Evelina bring the food on his trolley. But it would have to be on the last run when he was returning to the depot. It would be safer then because he would have no passengers. Any other time Santos would get caught using the trolley for personal business and lose his job.

Santos's last run was very late in the evening, long after the food center closed for the day. Once Evelina picked up the food, she would have a five-hour wait in the cold February weather. So now the problem was where to wait with the food until the trolley came.

 4   What are you thinking about now?

Evelina visited a church that was near the food distribution center. She spoke to the minister about her plan to collect food for the poor. "We need your help, sir," she declared. "I will be taking many shopping bags of food to give to poor and hungry families. We'll have to wait for five hours before we can take it away, and it's very cold. Please help."

The minister was very impressed with little Evelina. He agreed to help her and ordered the sexton to let them wait with the food in the church basement until Santos came.

The day arrived and Evelina rode free on Santos's trolley to the food distribution center. When she presented the stack of completed forms at the counter, all the workers were taken aback.

"Where are all the people who claim this food?" asked the supervisor, who had been quickly called to the counter by one of the workers.

"They are too ashamed to come," Evelina answered. "They feel like they are begging, so I have come to get their food for them."

"This is too irregular," said the supervisor, shaking his head. "I don't know."

 5 What do you think the supervisor is thinking about Evelina and her plan?

"Is there a law against this, sir? Doesn't the food belong to the people who filled out the forms? Isn't this food for poor families and their children?"

Evelina bombarded the supervisor with questions and statements.

"Plenty of people are starving and you have so much food here. If they can't come here to get it, then why can't I take it to them? Please, sir," she pleaded, "in the name of justice! It's the only way, and it must be allowed!"

"You're wearing me out!" the supervisor complained with a laugh. "But even if I give you all of these shopping bags, how will you get them out of here?"

"My uncle and my neighbor will be here in one hour to help. Then we are delivering the shopping bags to each and every one of these families. Right to their door," she told him, "like I have promised them. I may come back every month. *¿Pero, quién sabe?* But who knows? Maybe some of these families will come here for themselves next time. Only don't worry because the people will get their food."

All the employees came out to see who this girl with the pretty face and dark, curly hair was. Evelina smiled happily as she checked out all the food against the completed forms. Then she took each shopping bag and set it against the wall and waited until she saw Tío Godreau and Miriam. They had each brought an empty wagon to the center.

"You did it!" shouted Tío Godreau. Miriam hugged Evelina. "You are something special, little Miss Evelina!" she said.

 6   What do Tío Godreau and Miriam think about Evelina now?

All three loaded the shopping bags into the wagons. The wagons were not big enough to carry all twelve bags in one trip. So they made two trips to the nearby church before all the food was safely put into the church basement.

Then they waited for Santos and his trolley. Finally, in the darkness of night, they loaded the shopping bags onto the trolley. Santos shut off the lights inside the trolley. Then he told them that they must sit way in the back of the trolley.

"You three will have to keep down and stay out of sight," said Santos. "I'll be passing by all the trolley stops. But," he added nervously, "if another driver—or our dispatcher—sees you, I'll be in trouble. So stay low!"

Evelina, Tío Godreau, and Miriam sat scrunched down in the shadows at the back of the trolley. Each time they passed a trolley stop, they heard Santos say a prayer under his breath. When they finally reached 116th Street, Evelina felt a sense of relief just knowing that Cousin Santos would not be in trouble.

 7 What are you thinking about now?

That night Evelina, Tío Godreau, and Miriam went to the door of every family that had completed a form and distributed the food to them.

On her next trip to the distribution center, Evelina was not alone. She was joined by a group of neighbors, including Señor Sanchez.

"Evelina, you've given us courage," he told her. "From now on I'll be going to get my own food and so will the rest of us."

With each passing month, Evelina's task of collecting food became easier. More and more of her neighbors went to the distribution center with her.

 8   What do you conclude about what Evelina did?

Soon all her neighbors were seeking on their own the help they were entitled to. Evelina had shown her neighbors that there was no shame in accepting help when it was needed. Babies wouldn't cry through the night for food. Children wouldn't go to school hungry and with no energy to learn. And people working or looking for work wouldn't get sick because they didn't have enough food to eat.

Time to Write!

In the selection you just read, Evelina helps her neighbors improve their lives. Now you are going to write about a project you want to do to improve the place where you live or go to school.

- For this activity, you will write a letter to the mayor or principal about a project you want to do to improve your neighborhood, community, or school.

Prewriting

First, use the boxes below to help you organize your thoughts.

What is the problem you want to fix?

Why is it an important problem?

What can you do to help?

Writing

Now, use another sheet of paper to write a letter to the mayor or principal about the project you can do to help your neighborhood or school.

33

Your Own Opinion

Read the selection below. As you read, think about your opinion.

Anita didn't know what to do. Her new friend, Maria, had asked her to go to the fall festival. Anita really wanted to go. But Anita had already planned to go to a movie with her best friend, Helena. She enjoyed going to the movies each week with Helena, but the fall festival sounded exciting. She also wanted to spend time with her new friend. She knew if she went to the festival with Maria, Helena would be very hurt. It was a hard decision for Anita. What could she do to make everyone happy?

When you read the selection, you probably thought about many different things. Check the boxes next to what you thought about while you read.

I thought about

☐ how fun it would be to go to the festival.

☐ how I would feel if I were Anita.

☐ what I would do if I were Anita.

This made me think that I would like to go to the festival with both my friends.

What else did you think about while you read?

_____

_____

_____

_____

_____

Read and Think

- Read the selections that follow.
- Stop at each box and answer the question.
- Remember to think about your opinion as you read.

The Loch Ness Monster

By Brian Innes

Let's Read

This selection is about the legend of the Loch Ness monster. The Loch Ness monster is a creature some people claim to have seen in a lake in northern Scotland. Read the selection to find out about the Loch Ness monster.

Loch Ness is a long, narrow lake in the Great Glen, which cuts like a deep canyon across the Highlands of Scotland. The loch is 22 miles (35 km) long. It is more than 970 feet (297 m) deep, but it is less than 1 mile (1.6 km) wide.

The first known sighting of the Loch Ness monster was 1,500 years ago. St. Columba had set up a monastery on the island of Iona, off Scotland's west coast. From there, he traveled through the north of Scotland.

In 565, St. Columba came to Loch Ness. One of his followers, called Lugne, was bold enough to swim across the mouth of the Ness River. He wanted to take a boat from the other side. Suddenly he met a "very odd looking beastie, something like a huge frog, only it was not a frog." The monster opened its mouth. It swam to attack Lugne.

Seeing this, St. Columba raised his arms and shouted: "Go thou no farther, nor touch the man. Go back at once!" Then, according to the account, "on hearing this word, the monster was terrified and fled away again. . . ."

In Scotland, the monster was called "Niseag." This is a Scottish Gaelic word. Its English name was "Nessie." For centuries, local people lived in fear of the monster. Children were told not to play near the water. There were hundreds of descriptions of the beast.

Patrick Rose reported, in 1771, that he had seen something in the loch. He described it as half like a horse, and half like a camel. In 1880, Duncan McDonald was trying to raise a sunken boat. "I was underwater about my work," he said, "when all of a sudden the monster swam by me as cool and calm as you please." In 1907, a group of children saw Nessie. She was slipping into the water. They said the monster had four legs. She was light brown in color. She looked "like a camel."

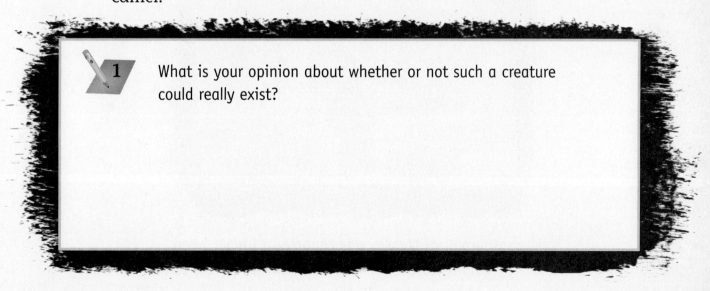

1 What is your opinion about whether or not such a creature could really exist?

For a few years, all seemed to be quiet. Then, on July 22, 1930, Ian Milne was fishing for salmon with two friends. They were in a small boat. Some 600 yards (546 m) away they suddenly saw spray being thrown high up into the air. A creature rushed toward them. It turned, then moved away again. It traveled at a speed of some 15 mph (24 kmph). "The part of it we saw would be about 20 feet [6 m] long. And it was standing 3 feet [90 cm] or so out of the water. The wash [waves] it created caused our boat to rock violently," reported Milne.

Until the 1930s the shores of Loch Ness were difficult to reach. Then, a new road was built along the north shore. Tourists began to arrive. Soon Nessie made the newspaper headlines. In spring, 1933, John Mackay and his wife told the *Inverness Courier* they had seen the monster for a minute or more. Mackay said the beast made the water "froth and foam." It had a very small head when compared to the size of its body. Three months later, on July 22, George Spicer and his wife were driving along the new road. Their car nearly hit a huge black beast with a long neck. It waddled through the undergrowth. Then, it went into the water.

This photograph of Nessie was reported to have been taken by Colonel Robert Wilson in 1934. However, some people now believe it is a fake.

Later the same year, on November 12, Hugh Gray was standing by the loch. He saw something large rise out of the water. So he took a photograph of it. He guessed it was 40 feet (12 m) long. He said it was gray, and had a very smooth, shiny skin. This was the first photograph ever taken of Nessie. It was printed in newspapers all over the world. However, it was very blurred.

The following year, on April 12, a clearer photograph appeared. It was taken by a London physician, Colonel Robert Wilson. The picture showed a creature with a big body, a long neck, and a small head. Nessie looked like the ancient water reptile known as a plesiosaur.

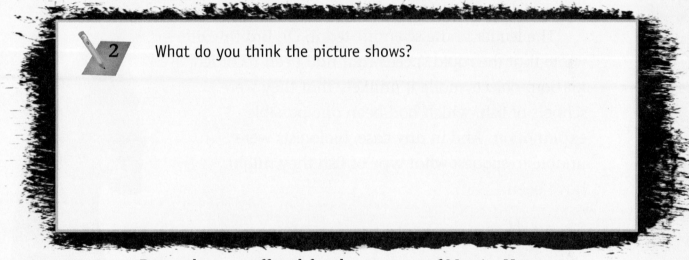

2   What do you think the picture shows?

Rewards were offered for the capture of Nessie. However, scientific experts were skeptical. At the British Museum, J. R. Norman stated: "The possibilities came down to the object being a bottlenose whale, one of the large species of shark, or just mere wreckage." He did not explain how a whale or shark could have gotten into Loch Ness.

A special "Loch Ness Investigation Bureau" was set up. Then, in 1960 and 1967, the monster was caught on film. Both films were blurred, but showed a fast-moving object leaving a wave behind it as it shot through the water. Experts suggested that this was caused by an otter. But the object's length above the loch's surface was about 7 feet (2.1 m). This was much longer than any otter.

On the evening of May 4, 1968, a number of people sighted what they thought was the monster. In August, a team from Birmingham University, England, set up a sonar scanner on a pier in Loch Ness. A sonar scanner is a machine that detects any sound made by moving objects. On August 28, they made a remarkable 13-minute recording.

A large object rose through the water from the bottom of the loch. It was about half a mile (800 m) away from them. It was traveling at a speed of around 100 feet (30 m) per minute, moving away from the pier. Then the object turned toward the pier again and dived deep. The sounds from a second object were recorded at the same time. The object dived at 450 feet (135 m) per minute.

The leader of the scientific team, Dr. Braithwaite, wrote that the rapid speeds that had been recorded for both objects made it unlikely that they were schools of fish, which had been one possible explanation. And in any case, biologists were unable to suggest what type of fish they might have been.

This model of the Loch Ness monster is based on eyewitness accounts. It looks somewhat like a plesiosaur.

It was not until 1970 that underwater photography was tried. Because the water was murky, this was difficult. But there were some interesting results. Dr. Robert Tines, a scientific expert from Boston, Massachusetts, was one of the most successful. He took photographs that showed some kind of animal fin. Later, something that looked like a complete long-necked creature was photographed.

Above water, visitors to Loch Ness continued to produce photographs they claim are of the monster surfacing. One of the most convincing was taken by Jennifer Bruce in 1982. She took a picture of the view across part of the loch. At the time she noticed nothing unusual. But, when the photograph was developed, it clearly showed a head and neck rising out of the water.

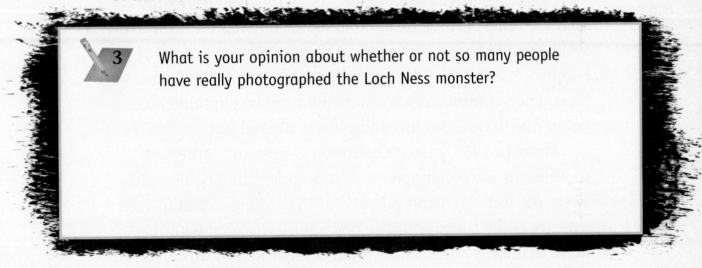

3 What is your opinion about whether or not so many people have really photographed the Loch Ness monster?

If there is a monster, or more than one, in Loch Ness, what can it be? Most descriptions are closest to that of a plesiosaur— a water reptile believed to have been extinct for the past 70 million years. Animals are said to be extinct, meaning that they have all died, once they have not been seen for a long time. But they may still exist. Until 1938, the coelacanth, a very ugly fish, was also said to have been extinct for 70 million years. Then fishermen started catching it in the Indian Ocean.

In 1987, Operation Deepscan attempted to solve the Loch Ness mystery. However, the fleet of 24 boats failed to find any trace of Nessie.

Nessielike monsters have also been reported in nearby lochs. Whatever these beasts are, teams of people continue to seek them. Between 1962 and 1977, six different groups of people used the most modern equipment to explore Loch Ness. They obtained results that could not be explained as being due to fish, nor anything like a sunken log.

Then, in 1987, came "Operation Deepscan." A fleet of motorboats, each equipped with sound-detecting equipment, swept the loch from end to end. But they found nothing. That was not really surprising. The boats filled the area with the noise of their engines. That would surely frighten any creature into hiding. So the search for Nessie continues.

4   What do you think the "truth" is about the Loch Ness monster?

Time to Write!

Imagine that you are an explorer in Loch Ness, Scotland. You have had an experience that convinces you that the Loch Ness monster does or does not exist.

• For this activity, you will write a persuasive paragraph to convince others that you are correct.

Prewriting

First, organize your thoughts by answering the questions below.

Which will you try to prove—that the Loch Ness monster does exist or does not exist?

_____

What experiences, facts, and reasons would prove or disprove the monster's existence?

_____

_____

_____

_____

_____

_____

Writing

Now, choose three of the most convincing ideas from your list. Use another sheet of paper to write your persuasive paragraph.

43

Shelly and the Great Purple Hairstreak

By Debbie A. Taylor

Let's Read

This selection is about a girl who loves to find butterflies. She has to decide how to enter a collection contest without harming the butterflies. Read to find out if her collection wins a ribbon.

"Got it!" The milky-winged butterfly fluttered to the top of Shelly's jar. Leaning against a tree, Shelly smiled as the sun warmed her face.

"Hey, Petey!" she yelled to her brother as he squatted on the ground looking for rocks. "I caught a cabbage butterfly!" she said, tucking the jar into her bag. She carefully stepped over an anthill.

"I found this!" Petey held up a speckled stone. "I'll have a great rock collection for the contest."

"Hey, there's Jamal's kite!" yelled Petey. Up, up soared the yellow kite, like a butterfly dancing in the wind. Jamal would enter his kite collection in the contest at the school tomorrow afternoon. Most everyone in the circle of houses was excited about the contest. And most everyone hoped to win a ribbon.

Dragonflies darted and two orange butterflies hovered overhead. While Petey poked around with a stick, Shelly caught a black swallowtail on thistles near the edge of the fields. She found holly blues on clover leaves close to a cluster of maple trees.

 1 Why do you think people enjoy collecting things?

"Shelly, will you keep these butterflies for tomorrow? You'd win a ribbon for sure."

"No. I'll release them today because butterflies don't live long. Last summer, I kept an orange sulfur all night. But the next morning, the wings were ragged, and orange smudges stuck to the glass. It just crawled through the grass and hid under a leaf."

Just then, the cabbage butterfly opened its wings.

"But I can find more tomorrow," Shelly continued. "I once caught two butterflies on one flower." They tromped through a patch of weeds. Something moved on a flower just ahead.

"Oooh. The wings are blue with little tails!" whispered Shelly.

No, the wings were purple. Shelly stared. Could it be? It was. A great purple hairstreak! Hairstreaks almost never came to their field of thistles, clover, and mint.

She took a deep breath and crept toward the butterfly. Slowly, slowly, she raised the jar. Then she lowered it. "Petey, it's a great purple hairstreak." Huge purple wings, streaked with black, shimmered in the jar.

 2   What are you thinking about now?

"A hairstreak!" she said softly. Shelly and Petey walked along slowly.

Deeper into the field, the mud was so sticky it spotted their shoes. Smuck-smuck. Petey poked his stick into a mud hole. Then . . . Buzz. Zzit. Zzit. Wasps swirled from the hole.

Zzzzit. Shelly slapped at the insect buzzing near her face. Petey dropped his stick and ran. Shelly felt a prick and looked down. Three wasps were stinging her ankle.

"Ouch!"

Shelly swatted at them as she tore through the field, scrambling through weeds and grass. Oh, I can't drop my bag, she thought. She ran across the backyard and tripped on the back porch.

"What's wrong?" asked her mother.

"Wasps!" Petey gasped.

Shelly looked down: the wasps were gone, but her ankle was swollen. In the living room, she plopped on the sofa.

"This ice should reduce the swelling," Mom said as she arranged an ice bag over Shelly's ankle. "Let's prop this foot on a pillow. Now, you need to stay out of the field tomorrow."

"But, Mom, I have to catch butterflies for my collection."

"Shelly, you stay out of the field," she repeated firmly. "But, you can go see the other collections."

---

3   Do you think Shelly's mom is being fair?

Shelly frowned as Petey pasted his speckled rock to a piece of cardboard. What can I do? Shelly wondered. I have a cabbage white, holly blues, a swallowtail—even a great purple hairstreak right now. She hugged her pillow and frowned. Maybe I'll just keep them overnight. After a while, she dozed off.

When she opened her eyes, the moonlight shined on the jars lining the floor.

"Oh," she gasped, jumping from the couch. Are their wings tattered? Peering into the jar, she could see the wings—purple, yellow, blue, and white. These butterflies can't stay in jars all night, she thought.

The flashlight beam lit up just part of the field as Shelly limped along. She unscrewed the lids and shook each jar gently. The cabbage butterfly flitted like a tiny ghost in the white light.

The holly blues disappeared into the grass. The swallowtail darted away. Up, up, up flew the great purple hairstreak, shimmering blue then purple, circling the tree. She kept the light beam on it as far as she could, then it vanished into the darkness.

Back inside, she sighed. No butterfly collection. She set the row of empty jars near Petey's crayons, tissue paper, scissors, and paste.

 4 Do you think Shelly did the right thing by letting the butterflies go?

"Hmm," she said, unfolding a square of tissue paper. Could I make a butterfly from this? She tossed the paper up. It swished, then swayed, and finally touched the floor. She worked for a long time, cutting and twisting and pasting.

Hours later, it was time to get to the school. Petey balanced his collection of rocks, while Shelly clutched a box. Long tables held posters and bottles and rocks and hats and other things. Elaina carried in a tray of erasers shaped like vegetables and fruit. Sherman's tooth collection filled a table. Dog tooth. Sherman's baby tooth. Shark tooth. Grizzly bear tooth. Iris's glass pigs posed on velvet squares, and stuffed pigs perched on the table edge. Wearing a collection of buttons, Martin skipped around. Simon's caps came from all over: Seattle, Miami, Toronto, Detroit, San Juan. A diamond kite dangled above Jamal's head. The box kite, as tall as Jamal, was propped against the table, and a sleek dragon kite draped the wall behind him.

Jamal looked up. "Did you bring your butterflies, Shelly?"

Shelly placed the box on the table. She lined up tissue butterflies one by one. Cabbage butterfly. Swallowtail. Holly blue. Great purple hairstreak.

Black spots on the cabbage butterfly looked like eyes. The swallowtail's streaked yellow and black wings spread wide. The holly blue's wings were tipped with ink. The largest butterfly glimmered: curved tails hung from the hind wings of the great purple hairstreak.

"Hmm." Walking around the hall, the judge tapped her plastic clipboard.

COLLECTION
CONTEST

TOOTH
COLLECTION

GLASS
PIG
COLLECTION

CAP
COLLECTION

KITE
COLLECTIO

49

The judge turned a page in a stamp album. Then she picked up a glass pig. She looked so closely at the butterflies that her nose almost touched one. The judge moved to the next table. Before long, she had stopped at every display. Finally, she marched to the middle of the room.

"Each collector will receive a ribbon," she announced, holding up a white ribbon. "Now for the awards. Third prize goes to the . . . pig collection." Iris beamed as she accepted the purple ribbon. "Second prize goes to the . . . cap collection. First prize goes to the . . . kite collection."

Shelly clapped for her friends.

"Finally, we have two awards for unusual collections. One goes to the tooth collection. The last award goes to the collection of paper butterflies."

Shelly squealed. "Yes!" Waving the silky green ribbon above her head, she grinned.

At home, Shelly, Jamal, and Petey sat on the back porch sipping lemonade.

"Next year," said Petey, "I'm going to collect postcards."

Shelly squinted at the holly blues and swallowtails dipping and dancing in the field.

"I'll help you, Petey," said Shelly. "And you can help me make a great purple hairstreak as big as Jamal's kite."

 5 What are you thinking about now?

Time to Write!

Imagine that you are entering a collection contest. Tell about a collection that you have or one that you would like to have.

- For this activity, you will write an essay about a collection that you would like to enter in a contest.

Prewriting

First, organize your thoughts by answering the questions below.

What do you collect? Or what would you like to collect? _____

When did you start your collection? _____

Why did you start your collection? _____

_____

_____

Describe your favorite item in your collection. Why is it your favorite?

_____

_____

_____

What else would you like people to know about your collection?

_____

_____

Writing

Now, use another sheet of paper to write your essay.

51

Giant Pandas

By John Bonnett Wexo

Let's Read

This selection describes Giant Pandas, where they live, what they look like, and what they eat. Read the selection to find out what is special about Giant Pandas.

Giant Pandas are among the most beautiful and rare animals in the world. They are near the top of almost everybody's list of favorite animals. Whenever there are Giant Pandas in a zoo, people flock to see them.

1 What are you thinking about now?

52

It's easy to see why they are so popular. They look like big and cuddly Teddy bears, with soft black-and-white fur. They seem friendly and harmless, and even a little helpless at times. It almost seems like Giant Pandas were *made* for people to love.

Giant Pandas can be large animals, as their name implies. When fully grown, they can be almost 5 feet long, and they usually weigh over 200 pounds. The biggest Giant Panda ever weighed was almost 400 pounds. But Giant Pandas aren't really giants in the same way that an elephant is a giant. One average elephant weighs more than *thirty* Giant Pandas.

2   Why do you think these pandas are referred to as "giants"?

All of the wild Giant Pandas in the world live in western China. They are found in dense bamboo forests high up in the mountains. The forests are so dense that it has always been hard for people to find out much about wild pandas. The pandas stay hidden in the forest most of the time, where people can't even see them. In many ways, the Giant Panda is still a mysterious animal.

The Chinese people are very proud that these beautiful animals are found only in their country. They have even made the Giant Panda a symbol for their country, in the same way that the Bald Eagle is a symbol for the United States. The Chinese call the Giant Panda *daxiong mao* (dah-shohng mah-oo), which means "large cat-bear."

 3 What are you thinking about now?

The people of China are doing many things to protect their Giant Pandas. They have set aside areas of wild land as panda reserves. Chinese scientists are working with scientists from other countries to find out more about wild pandas. And it is against the law in China to harm a Giant Panda in any way.

Many zoos would like to have pandas because they are so popular with zoo visitors. But only a few zoos outside China are allowed to have them, because they are an endangered species.

Giant Pandas are mysterious. Nobody is really sure what kind of animal they are. Some scientists say that the Giant Panda is a member of the *raccoon* family. But others claim that it belongs to the *bear* family. And a third group is sure that it doesn't belong to *either* family.

Raccoon

Red Panda

Scientists who say that Giant Pandas are raccoons try to prove it by showing that the Giant Panda is closely related to a small animal called the *Red Panda*. Many people believe that the Red Panda belongs to the raccoon family. So, if the Giant Panda and the Red Panda are related, and the Red Panda is a raccoon . . . well, the Giant Panda must also be a raccoon.

4 Why do you think scientists are not sure if the Giant Panda is a member of the raccoon family or the bear family?

But scientists who claim that Giant Pandas are bears don't agree that the Giant Panda and the Red Panda are closely related. As you will see on these pages, there seem to be plenty of facts to prove that Giant Pandas are bears . . . or maybe raccoons . . . or maybe something else. It's all very confusing.

Giant Pandas may be *bears* because . . . newborn bears and newborn Giant Pandas look very much alike. Both are very tiny compared to their parents, and both are covered with very fine hair.

Giant Pandas may be *bears* because . . . Giant Pandas look like bears. They have big round bodies like bears, and big round heads. The ears on Giant Pandas even look like the ears of Asiatic Black Bears, which live in the same part of the world.

 5 What do you think are good reasons that some scientists believe the Giant Panda is a member of the bear family?

Asiatic Black Bear   **Giant Panda**

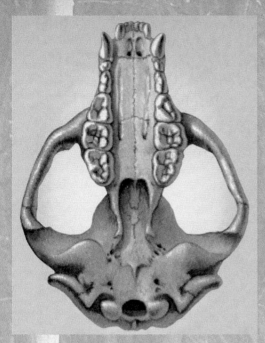

Giant Panda

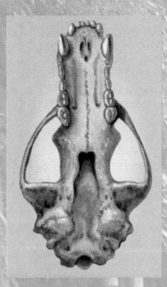

Polar Bear

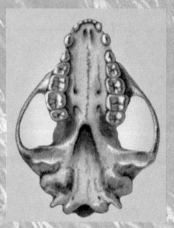

Red Panda

Giant Pandas may be *raccoons* because . . . the teeth of Giant Pandas and Red Pandas are very much alike. And the teeth of Giant Pandas are very *different* from bear teeth. Bears have narrow teeth that are made for cutting and chewing. But Giant Pandas and Red Pandas have wide teeth that are made for crushing bamboo.

Giant Pandas may be *raccoons* because . . . Red Pandas and Giant Pandas both eat a lot of bamboo. They bring the bamboo up to their mouths in a similar way. And they use their teeth to strip off the hard outer covering of the bamboo in a similar way.

Giant Pandas may not be bears or raccoons because . . . Giant Pandas sit down to eat their food, but bears and Red Pandas do not. And only the Giant Panda has special "thumbs" for grabbing things tightly.

The scientific evidence is *confusing* . . . Some blood tests have indicated that Giant Pandas are more closely related to bears than to Red Pandas. But studies of panda genetics seem to show that the Giant Panda is most closely related to the Red Panda.

6   What are you thinking about now?

The future of Giant Pandas is hard to predict. They are already among the most endangered animals on earth, and their numbers are very small. Scientists believe that there may be less than 1,000 Giant Pandas still living in the mountains of western China.

To survive, these wild pandas will need enough land to live on, and enough bamboo to eat. The Chinese government has already done a great deal to help give the pandas these things. Large areas have been set aside as panda reserves—and these areas contain some of the best bamboo forest remaining in China.

But the pandas are still not totally safe. There are people living in some of the reserves, and they want to cut down more bamboo to make room for farming. Other people would like to cut down the trees and bamboo in the forest to build houses.

The most serious danger for pandas may come from the *bamboo plants* that pandas like to eat. Each kind (or species) of bamboo plant lives and grows for a certain number of years—from 40 to 80 years. Then the bamboo plants of that species flower and die. When one species of bamboo dies, *all* of the bamboo of that kind dies *at the same time*. Entire forests of bamboo may die all at once, leaving the pandas that live in those forests without bamboo to eat.

7 What do you think is the most serious threat to the survival of the Giant Panda?

This happened in 1975, when all of the Umbrella Bamboo died. With nothing to eat, more than 150 Giant Pandas starved to death. In 1983, all of the Arrow Bamboo died, and hundreds of pandas were in danger again. But this time, the Chinese and the World Wildlife Fund were able to help the pandas.

For several years, Chinese scientists and World Wildlife Fund scientists have been studying pandas and their food supply. They hope to learn enough to make sure that wild pandas will always have enough living space and enough to eat. And they want to find ways to increase the number of pandas that are born in the wild and in zoos. If they can do all of these things, the future of Giant Pandas may be bright after all.

 8 What do you think is the future of the Giant Panda?

Time to Write!

Think about your favorite kind of animal. It might be a wild animal, farm animal, or a pet.

• For this activity, you will write an article about your favorite animal for a classroom magazine.

Prewriting

First, answer the questions below.

What animal are you going to write about? _____
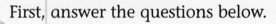
What does the animal look like? _____

_____

Where does the animal live? _____

_____

What does the animal eat? _____

_____

What is special about the animal? _____

_____

_____

Writing

Now, use another sheet of paper to write about the animal.

61

You have been thinking along as you read. Now practice thinking along to help you answer test questions.

Read and Think

- Read each selection.
- Stop at each box and answer the question.
- Answer the questions at the end of each selection.

Why did Ginny win an award?

Ginny was not sure why she was getting so much attention from all of the people milling around on the floor below the platform. It was comforting to be next to Philip.

She wasn't used to crowds, nor to those terrible flashes coming from the boxes some people were holding. Once in a while she would get up on all fours, trying to get closer to Philip.

To one side of Philip sat a man with a cat in his lap. People came up and petted it and called it "Cleo." There were many cats in this room, but not one other dog. Ginny didn't mind that. She preferred cats to dogs, actually. There were lots of cats at home. She shared everything with them.

 1   **What are you thinking about now?**

A reporter approached them. Ginny felt Philip straighten up.

"How old is Ginny?" the reporter asked. She held out a microphone.

"She's ten," replied Philip.

"What breed is she?"

"She is part schnauzer and part Siberian husky."

"How does she feel about all this?" the reporter asked, patting Ginny's head.

"She thinks everyone may be a bit confused," Philip said, with a soft laugh.

Soon a lady stood in front of them and began talking. The people below became quiet. The lady pointed to Cleo. "It is my honor to welcome Cleo, last year's Westchester Feline Club's 'Cat of the Year.'" There was applause, startling Ginny a bit. The man holding Cleo stood up. "And now," the lady said, "we come to the highlight of the afternoon— this year's winner." A murmur flowed through the audience.

"Selecting the cat of the year," the lady said, "is not an easy task. There were over three hundred entrants this year. The award goes each year to a cat who displays unusual courage, determination, the will to live, or other qualities not taken into account in the judging rings of our cat show. Cleo has those. She had to learn to eat through a straw.

"The title this year goes to Ginny, who shares her life with many cats and Philip Gonzalez of Long Beach, Long Island. Mr. Gonzalez adopted Ginny from an animal shelter. He has placed hundreds of cats in good homes. Others that could not be placed live with him and Ginny."

On hearing her name echoing in the big room, Ginny's ears perked up.

"Ginny welcomes all the cats who live at her house while Philip finds a home for them. And she goes out and finds cats who need help. Ginny is always bringing home stray cats who need a trip to the vet, a good meal, and a home.

"It is my pleasure," the lady went on, turning toward Ginny and Philip, "to introduce Ginny, this year's 'Cat of the Year.'" Applause rang out as Philip stood up and led Ginny to where the lady stood. Cameras flashed all around the room.

 2   What are you thinking about now?

The lady pinned a ribbon on Philip's coat. Philip took something from her and then lifted Ginny to a table beside him. He held what the lady had given him in front of Ginny's face. She couldn't read, of course. But she knew something big was happening, and she and Philip were at the center of it.

Philip leaned into the microphone. "Ginny says 'Thanks,'" he said. The man holding Cleo brought her up to congratulate Ginny, who gave Cleo a big kiss. The people applauded even louder. So Ginny barked.

"Well," Philip said, "Ginny says it's time to go home. We have a house full of guests to feed. And Ginny is eager to go look for more."

As Philip and Ginny left the stage, the people applauded the dog that had just been named "Cat of the Year."

 3 What are you thinking about now?

Darken the circle before the correct answer.

1. **Why does a dog win a "Cat of the Year" award?**
   - Ⓐ The judges thought she was a cat.
   - Ⓑ She had been raised by a cat.
   - Ⓒ She helped many cats.
   - Ⓓ The award really went to her friend Cleo.

2. **How does Ginny really feel about cats?**
   - Ⓐ She loves them.
   - Ⓑ They frighten her.
   - Ⓒ They confuse her.
   - Ⓓ She is jealous of them.

3. **The award is given every year by _____.**
   - Ⓐ Philip Gonzalez
   - Ⓑ the Westchester Feline Club
   - Ⓒ a newspaper
   - Ⓓ the city of Long Beach, Long Island

4. **What happens to most of the cats that Ginny brings home?**
   - Ⓐ They are given to the Westchester Feline Club.
   - Ⓑ They end up back on the street without a home.
   - Ⓒ They are taught to behave like dogs.
   - Ⓓ They move on to new homes Philip finds for them.

Write your answer on the lines below.

5. **Why do you think Philip received a ribbon?**

_____

_____

_____

_____

_____

Would you like to produce a class newspaper?

Did you know that some classes have their own newspaper? If you are interested in producing one, you should know that it can be a lot of work! It takes planning and time. But it is also fun.

Follow these seven steps to publish your first issue.

1. **Obtain permission to publish a newspaper.**

Talk to your teacher about your idea. Your teacher will need to review everything that you put in your newspaper.

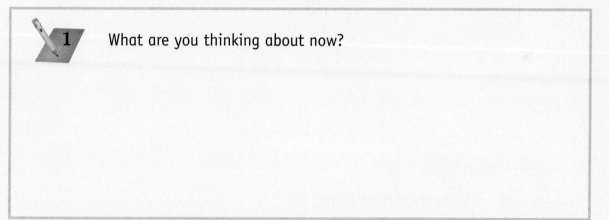

1 What are you thinking about now?

2. **See if the newspaper can be produced in your school.**

How are you going to produce your paper? You can't make all the copies by hand! You may need to find an adult sponsor. Is there a computer you can use? Is there a printer or copier you can use? Is there a camera available?

3. **Find out how much it will cost to produce the newspaper.**

What will it cost for paper, printer ink or toner, and any other materials? Where will you get money? Will you be allowed to charge your readers? Will you sell ads? Will you have a bake sale or raise money another way?

4. Think about who will read your newspaper, what you will call it, and how often it will come out.

This is a very important consideration. Who will read your paper? *You* will, of course, but how about other students in other classes in your school, your parents, other family members, and friends and neighbors outside of school? Pick a name for your newspaper that people will remember easily. How often do you think your publication should come out? You can produce the first issue and see how long it takes before you decide.

2 What are you thinking about now?

5. Plan your first issue.

This is the most important step of all. To make it easier, break it down into these substeps:

A. Decide the stories you want to have in the first issue. You can tell about what you are studying in class and special projects your class is doing. You can write about members of your class. What else would you like to feature? What pictures will you use? Make a list.

B. Assign tasks. Give particular stories to writers. Decide who will edit those stories. Who will draw or take the pictures? Who is going to do the typing? Who will lay the paper out (arrange all the stories on the pages)?

Who will do the printing? Make a list and put names beside the jobs.

C. Schedule production by starting with the date you want the paper to come out. Then work backwards. When will the editors need to get the "copy" to the people laying out and printing the paper? When will the writers need to get their stories to the editors? Put due dates beside the names on the list you made.

6. Now do it!

Follow your plans to produce your paper. Keep notes on problems that you have. See how close you can come to getting the paper out on time.

7. See if your readers can help you improve your paper.

Talk to your readers after they have seen the paper. Find out what they like best and what they would like to see in the next issue. Then get everyone in the class together to look at your notes and share ideas. Was the first issue a success? Do you want to continue publishing a paper? If so, what can you do to make the next issue better?

 3   What are you thinking about now?

Darken the circle before the correct answer.

6. The first step in planning a class paper requires getting _____.

    A story ideas

    B approval

    C readers

    D money

8. In the last step, you are looking for ways to _____.

    A improve your paper

    B avoid hard work

    C cause problems

    D print the paper by hand

7. The second and third steps relate to _____.

    A ways to produce the paper

    B what readers think of the paper

    C when things will be done

    D who will write the stories

9. In step 5, you are basically _____.

    A making copies of the paper

    B getting your teacher to help

    C making assignments

    D talking to your readers

Write your answer on the lines below.

10. Give two reasons why you would or would not like to produce your own class newspaper.

_____

_____

_____

_____

How does the class like its winter windows?

The windows along the side of Mrs. Minoru's classroom looked out over a grassy lawn in front of the school. From inside the room, the students could see beautiful palm trees swaying slightly in the wind. It was almost always a sunny, pleasant sight to see.

Keichi looked out at the trees sometimes. So did Mikallia. Annette looked out often. Mrs. Minoru had to call on her when she saw Annette daydreaming for too long, just to get Annette's mind back on her studies.

One day after the class had been studying geography and reading about life in Alaska, Finland, and other northern climates, Benny Barnham had an idea. "I was thinking," he said, "how nice it would be to look outside and see snow for a change."

"Yes," Mrs. Minoru said. "That would be interesting. But if you lived where that is all you saw for several months, you would long for our wonderful weather."

1   What are you thinking about now?

"But in Minnesota, for example," Annette said, "you could see big oak trees and maples, and lots of other kinds of trees—not just palms."

"They'd be bare, though," Keichi said. "They lose their leaves in winter."

Mrs. Minoru had an idea. "What do you think of this?" she said. "Pick a place with long winters and find pictures of it. Then you can paint pictures of that place across our windows. We'll use a water-based paint, so it will wash off more easily."

The class was excited, and Keichi had a suggestion. "We could show what people there do in the winter. Each window could show something people do in the snow."

It was decided. Each of the different teams was assigned a window. Annette's team painted children building a snowman. Keichi's team painted a hockey game on a frozen lake. Another group extended the lake onto another window to paint people ice skating.

On a fourth window, Benny's team painted a mountainside with skiers. The students found pictures that showed the kinds of clothes people wear and the details they needed to show each activity accurately. Some of the scenes had green pine trees. Some had different kinds of trees with snow on their bare branches.

 2 What are you thinking about now?

When the pictures were finished, all the windows looked like one big, wide picture—a panorama of winter. Other classes came by to see the windows. Several weeks passed. "It is very refreshing," Annette kept saying.

"Well, yes," Benny said. "It was at first."

"He's right," Keichi said. "All those trees were fun to see at first. But they don't move in the wind, the way our palms do. When will we wash the paint off the windows?"

"When everyone wants to see our sunny Hawaii again," Mrs. Minoru said. The class discussed it and decided that they had grown tired of winter and had begun to long for their real view again. Some volunteers came to school the next Saturday morning and washed the paint off the windows. Mrs. Minoru helped.

"It was nice seeing some snow," Benny said the next Monday. "But there is nothing like our wonderful palms. We never know how lucky we are until we try to change our beautiful weather."

 3 What are you thinking about now?

Darken the circle before the correct answer.

11. The students in this story live in

_____.

Ⓐ Minnesota

Ⓑ Finland

Ⓒ Hawaii

Ⓓ Alaska

13. Why do the students paint the windows?

Ⓐ The paint on them is peeling.

Ⓑ They want a change of scenery.

Ⓒ They want to hide the bad weather outside.

Ⓓ There is nothing to see outside the windows.

12. Which of the students daydreams most often?

Ⓐ Annette

Ⓑ Keichi

Ⓒ Benny

Ⓓ Mikallia

14. The word panorama in this story means _____.

Ⓐ a snowy hill

Ⓑ something to hold paint

Ⓒ a kind of tree

Ⓓ a wide picture

Write your answer on the lines below.

15. What lesson do you think the students learned from their window-painting project?

_____

_____

_____

_____

_____

Descriptive Language

Read the selection below. As you read, think about descriptive language.

Early one morning, Tomiko noticed dew on every single blade of grass. She said, "The dew sparkles like tiny diamonds sprinkled all over grassy slopes." Another time, as she watched the rain, she said, "The rain is coming down in buckets!" On a sunny day, Tomiko thought that the flowers looked as bright as the colored markers she used at school. Every time she looked out her window, Tomiko tried to paint pictures using words to describe what she saw.

When you read the selection, you probably thought about Tomiko's choice of words. Check the boxes next to what you thought of as you read. Then use your own words to describe each object.

This story made me think about using interesting language for descriptions.

I thought of

☐ a drop of water. _____

☐ a sudden rainstorm. _____

☐ a flower garden. _____

What else did you think of while you read?

_____

_____

_____

_____

_____

Read and Think

- Read the selections that follow.
- Stop at each box and answer the question.
- Remember to think about descriptive language as you read.

July Is a Mad Mosquito

By J. Patrick Lewis

Let's Read

This selection is a collection of poems about different months. Read the poems and think about how the poet describes the different months.

January

The snowshoe rabbit
    Sees the grouse
Hiding beside
    His snowshoe house—
A country dressed
    In winter white
Is best for keeping
    Out of sight.

1   What does the phrase "a country dressed in winter white" mean?

78

Raw days like these
No sparrow dares;
The month is made
For polar bears
And timber wolves.
Great days of ice!
Refrigerated
Paradise.

 2 Does January make you think of "refrigerated paradise"?

March

One day this coldhearted guest
Blusters in and thumps his chest,
Bends
    the
        birches
            to
                their
                    knees,
Nips the buds off all the trees.

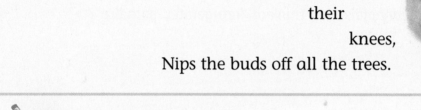

3   Who is the "coldhearted guest"?

Chickadees, two chipper chaps,
Trimmed in coal black bibs and caps,
Hop across the heather row,
Chirping *"Tut-tut-tut!"* to snow.

                  climb!
            to
        start
     may
Temperatures
Crocuses poke up in time.
March, the bullyboy, leaves town
Once the weather settles down.

April

My windowpane,
Blue-rinsed with rain,
Looks out on new
Grass wet with dew—
Earthworms crawl plain-
Ly into view.

And unaware
Of danger there,
Two earthworms cling
To leafy spring—
Which makes a pair
Of robins sing!

 4 Why do the robins sing?

June

Sunny bee, Honey bee
Nectar Inspector drops
Into my garden for
Peony tea—

Sipping sweet drinks on a
Hot afternoon takes the
Sting out of summer for
Me and the bee.

5   What is the "sting of summer" in this poem?

September

They've closed the public
    Swimming pool,
And children swarm
    Like fish to school.

6   Why do you think the poet compares the children to fish?

The bright orange bus
    Revs up, but boys
And girls outshout
    The engine noise.

Late summer skies
    Wind-whistle songs.
Dry heat heads south
    Where it belongs—

On city streets
    And rural routes
Where folks still wear
    Their bathing suits.

November

The bottoms of autumn
Wear diamonds of frost;
The tops of the trees rue
The leaves that they've lost.

7 Why do you think the author calls them "diamonds of frost"?

Red squirrels, busy packing
Oak cupboards for weeks,
Still rattle the branches
With seeds in their cheeks.

Gray clouds go on promising
Winter's first storm,
So we stay inside by
The stove to keep warm.

Home biscuits are baking,
The gravy is stirred,
Two pumpkin pies cool
By the thank-you bird.

Time to Write!

You have read several poems about different months of the year.

- For this activity, you will write your own poem that describes one month of the year. Remember, a poem doesn't have to rhyme.

Prewriting

First, think about your poem.

What month do you want to write about? _____

What is the weather like in that month?

_____

_____

What do you like to do in that month?

_____

_____

Does that month make you think of anything else?

_____

_____

_____

Writing

Now, use another sheet of paper to write your own poem about a month.

87

SKYSKATER

By T. C. Roth

This selection is about a girl and a boy who spend a day together skating. Read the selection and think about the winter day described in the story.

One year winter came early, caught the sky by surprise, and froze it into the surface of the pond where it had been lying on the water, kind of sleeping, I suppose.

1 What does the first line of this story tell you?

Strawberry was the first to discover it with his big blue eyes that never missed a beat and sometimes seemed to be looking right through you.

2 What does the description of his eyes tell you about Strawberry?

"Look at this," he called from the other end of the pond. I had already finished practicing my figures and was beginning to work on my routine. I thought at first that he was just fooling around, the way he always did when he didn't feel like practicing.

"What is it?" I said in a flat, tired voice.

"Just look!" he yelled back. So I skated to his side and looked down his pointing finger, half expecting to see a dead fish frozen under the surface, or something just as gross.

"At what?" I said, a little angry this time.

"Can't you see it?" he said.

I could feel his gaze on my cheek, as soft and warm as sunshine. "No," I said, biting my lip and looking harder. I couldn't see it. He had done this to me once before, in the summer, and when I had leaned over the bank and looked in the water, all I could see was my reflection shimmering back at me. Strawberry had said, "See! I told you there was a mermaid in the canal," and I had blushed hot and turned to hit him, but he was already running away through the tall grass in a spray of grasshoppers.

This time he put his hand on my shoulder and said, "It's the sky; it's frozen under the ice. Don't look so hard and you'll see it."

I squinted my eyes and cocked my head, and after a bit I began to see it, too. It was a beautiful deep blue sky, endless as the ocean, with white puffs of clouds that sailed across it like the ships of old. And it was captured beneath the surface of the ice like a September day frozen in time. It was so beautiful, I wished I were inside it.

3   What are you thinking about now?

I turned suddenly and caught Strawberry staring at me. "What are you looking at?" I said. For several slow seconds it seemed as though he were reading my mind, and then he looked away and the feeling passed.

"I was just thinking," he said, looking at his feet, "that maybe today we could skate together."

I looked at him, dumbfounded, and my mouth fell open. Just last winter I had suggested the same thing and he'd called me a sissy, then gave me a lecture about getting sweet on him. Then he had skated off in a huff and hadn't shown up to practice for three weeks.

But this time was different. "You're serious?" I said, squinting into the bright sunshine that shone from the white snow all around like a thousand spotlights.

"Let's go," he said, taking me by the hand and pulling me out to the center of the sky. His hair was red and his cheeks were red like a cherub's, and when he pressed his hand into mine, my skates sprouted wings. We swooped and spun and flew across the ice, and the wind roared in my ears.

4 What does she mean when she says her "skates sprouted wings"?

"Strawberry," I said, "I want to do a flying vee." The wind grabbed at my breath and pulled at my hair with small grasping hands.

 5 How does the wind make her feel?

"Then pretend you're floating across the sky, light as a cloud," he said, and I did, and it worked. I had never done that before.

"Strawberry," I said, "I want to do a double axel."

"Then pretend you're soaring on angel's wings, toward the sun," he said, and I did. And do you know what? For one brief glorious second, I really, really believed that I was an angel soaring to the sun, soaring and spinning and flashing through the air. And then the moment passed. I fell from the sky into a snowbank as soft as a cloud, where I sat panting and dazed, trying to catch my breath.

"Are you OK?" he asked, and I nodded, round-eyed. "You did it," he said.

"Yes," I said, smiling proudly and gasping. "But, Strawberry, then what happened? Why did I fall?"

"It's the sky," he said, "it's all gone." And when I got to my feet and joined him, I saw that, sure enough, it was. The passing of our skates had slashed and sliced and cut the ice to ribbons, and the sky had disappeared.

I hung my head sadly. "I'll never be able to skate like that again," I said.

"You'll never know until you try," Strawberry said,
smiling and reaching for my hand and looking right through
me with those eyes as big and bright and blue as my lost sky.

 6   How does she feel about Strawberry?

Time to Write!

This selection describes a special winter day. Think about a special day you have had. It could be a day that you did something really well or that you spent time with someone special to you.

• For this activity, you will write a journal entry about a special day you had.

Prewriting

First, think about your special day.

What special day do you want to write about?

_____

What did you do on this special day? _____

_____

_____

_____

Why was this special to you? _____

_____

_____

_____

Writing

Now, use another sheet of paper to write your journal entry about your special day.

HOOPS

Written by Robert Burleigh

Illustrated by Stephen T. Johnson

Let's Read

This selection is about basketball. It tells about the thoughts and ideas of the people playing the game. Read the selection to see how the writer describes the game of basketball and the players.

Hoops.
   The game.
      Feel it.

The rough roundness.
The ball
like a piece
of the thin long reach
of your body.

1 How can the ball be "like a piece of the thin long reach of your body"?

The way it answers whenever you call.
The never-stop back and forth flow,
like tides going in, going out.

2 What does the author try to tell the reader by making a comparison to tides?

The smooth,
skaterly glide
and sudden swerve.

The sideways slip
through a moment of narrow space.

The cool.

The into
and under
and up.

100

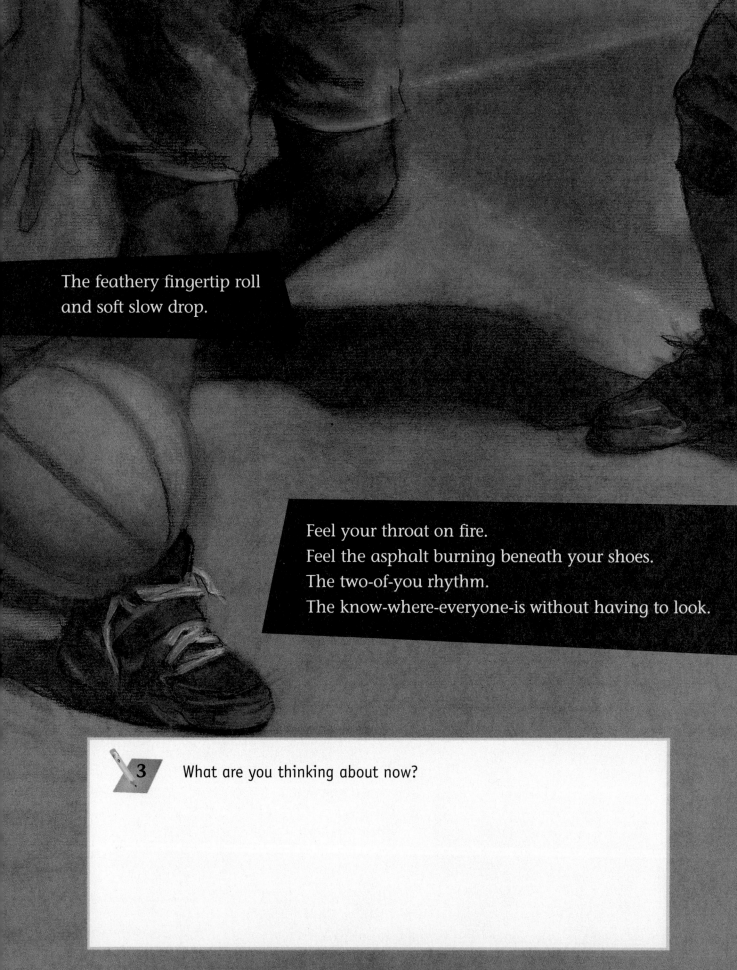

The feathery fingertip roll
and soft slow drop.

Feel your throat on fire.
Feel the asphalt burning beneath your shoes.
The two-of-you rhythm.
The know-where-everyone-is without having to look.

3   What are you thinking about now?

The watching
and waiting
to poke
and pounce.

The fox on the lurk.

The hunger.

4 What is the player hungry for?

The leap from the pack.

The out-in-the-clear
like a stallion
with wind in your face.

The bent legs tense
as the missed shot swirls
and silently spins.

104

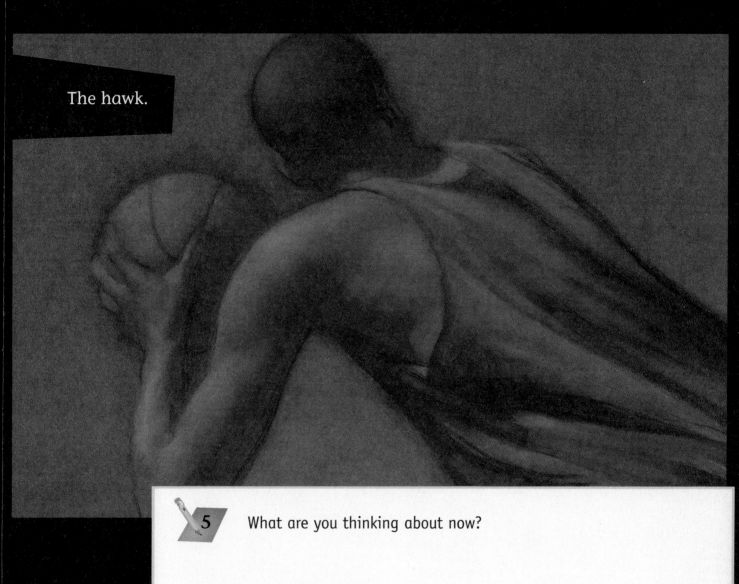

The hawk.

5   What are you thinking about now?

Your arm shooting up
through a thicket of arms.

The lean
and brush
and burst free.

The skittery,
cat-footed dance
along the baseline.

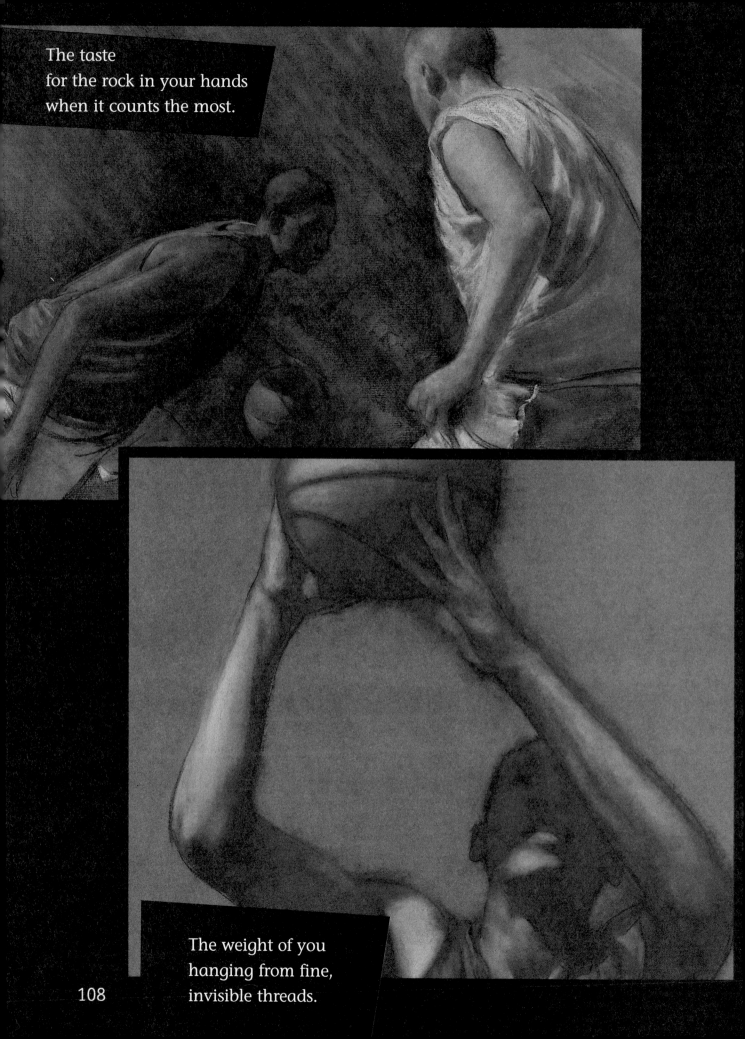

The taste
for the rock in your hands
when it counts the most.

108

The weight of you
hanging from fine,
invisible threads.

The eyes.

as it sinks
through nothing but still,
pure air.
Yes.

 6   What sound is "the no-sound sound of the ball"?

Hoops.
The game.
Feel it.

7 What are you thinking about now?

Time to Write!

Think about a sport or game that you like to play. Write a descriptive paragraph or poem. Include interesting words and phrases to help make the reader feel the sport or game. Your poem can rhyme, or it can be unrhymed like "Hoops."

• For this activity, you will write a descriptive paragraph or poem.

Prewriting

First, use the idea web below to brainstorm ideas and vivid and interesting words and phrases.

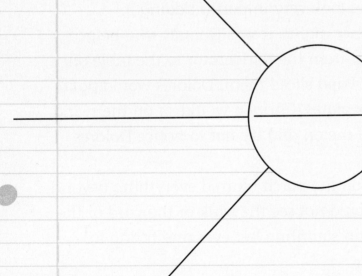

Writing

Now, use another sheet of paper to write your paragraph or poem about a favorite sport or game.

You have been thinking along as you read. Now practice thinking along to help you answer test questions.

Read and Think

- Read each selection.
- Stop at each box and answer the question.
- Answer the questions at the end of each selection.

What does Carmen want?

Carmen worried that her sister, Dolores, was her father's favorite. When they went to the fair to celebrate Cinco de Mayo, Papa would ask Dolores to go with him to buy tacos for the whole family. She would carry one of the boxes back to the picnic table and look very important doing it.

On hot, dry summer nights, it was Dolores who helped bring the watermelons from the refrigerator to the table on the front porch. After Papa sliced them, Dolores would put them on strong paper plates. Carmen would sit on the swing munching her slice of melon and try not to notice Dolores assisting Papa.

The bright lights on the porch blurred everything beyond them, and Carmen could not see the walk or the yard or the fence clearly. It was fun squinting her eyes and trying to make out details.

Then the porch would become a stage. Out there were all her fans—Papa among them. Her friend Vilma was there, too, waving at Carmen. Vilma was an only child. She knew she was *her* father's favorite.

1 What are you thinking about now?

Carmen wanted to think she was Papa's favorite. But at Padre Island, where the family went for vacation, it was Dolores who stood by Papa as he posed with the big fish he had caught. Papa had the photograph enlarged, and it hung on the kitchen wall for many years. Sometimes the picture seemed to be saying "Papa's Favorite" to Carmen.

Carmen wanted Papa to put her picture on the wall. Sometimes she would close her eyes and see a colorful poster in another frame on the wall. Her face was on it, and it said "Carmen Delgado in Concert."

Carmen knew that her father loved her—and Luis, her brother, too. Papa taught Luis how to do many things. Papa was very proud of Carmen. When he spoke to her, she knew that she was very special to him. But she worried that Dolores was even more special than she was. And even though her mother understood her feelings and tried to make it up to her, Carmen still worried.

"But I worry that you are Mama's favorite," Dolores said one day when Carmen complained to her about the extra attention she thought Dolores got from Papa. "Mama is always listening to you play and sing your songs," Dolores said.

2 What are you thinking about now?

Dolores and Carmen were out in the yard with the porch light off so they could look at all the stars in the sky. "I wish I had a dream like yours," Dolores said. Carmen knew what worried Dolores. Mama was always helping Carmen dream about her music and about how one day she would sell millions of CDs and stand on a stage singing in front of thousands of adoring fans.

"Poor Luis," Carmen said. "If you think I am Mama's favorite, and I think you are Papa's favorite, whose favorite is he?"

"He is everyone's favorite," Dolores said. "Yours, mine, everyone's. After all, he is the only brother and son in the house." They both sat hugging their knees and gazing at the night sky.

"Which star is yours, Carmen?" The deep, soft voice came from behind them in the dark. It was Papa.

"All of them, Papa. All of them are mine!"

"I believe it," he said simply. "I hope every one of them is a wish that will come true." Then he started singing in his own soft way. "A special wish-come-true for my special Carmen," he sang. He and Dolores and Carmen all laughed gently in the dark.

3   What are you thinking about now?

Darken the circle before the correct answer.

1. Carmen hopes that someday she will
   be a famous _____.
   - Ⓐ photographer
   - Ⓑ cook
   - Ⓒ singer
   - Ⓓ dreamer

3. The front porch becomes a stage when
   _____.
   - Ⓐ Carmen imagines she is performing
   - Ⓑ the family vacations on Padre Island
   - Ⓒ Carmen is with her family during Cinco de Mayo
   - Ⓓ the sisters are wishing on the stars

2. Who does Carmen think is "Papa's
   favorite"?
   - Ⓐ Luis
   - Ⓑ Dolores
   - Ⓒ Carmen
   - Ⓓ Vilma

4. How does Carmen's father feel about
   her dream?
   - Ⓐ He thinks it is foolish.
   - Ⓑ He hopes it will come true.
   - Ⓒ He thinks Dolores should have it.
   - Ⓓ He doesn't know she has it.

Write your answer on the lines below.

5. How does Carmen feel about Dolores? How do you know?

_____

_____

_____

_____

What did Bette Bao Lord write?

Writers often write about their personal experiences. Bette Bao Lord is a writer who does just that. She writes about China, and some of her books are for young readers. She wrote a book called *In the Year of the Boar and Jackie Robinson*. It is not Bette Bao Lord's autobiography, but it is closely based on her life as a young girl.

The girl in the book is Bandit Wong, who comes to Brooklyn, New York, in 1947 with her family. That is just what happened to Bette. She came with her mother to join her father, who was in the United States buying equipment needed to rebuild China after World War II. Sansan, a younger sister of Bette's, was left behind with friends in China.

Like the character she creates, Bette had a lot to learn to get along in Brooklyn. She couldn't speak a word of English. Everything about life in America seemed very different to her. That is what happens to Bandit in the book.

To survive at school, Bandit has to learn fast. Making new friends is slow and difficult. But Bandit Wong, who becomes known as Shirley Temple Wong, is brave and determined. She begins to learn the new language, and soon she has a best friend.

 1 What are you thinking about now?

This is where Jackie Robinson comes in. One of the first things that Shirley Temple Wong falls in love with in Brooklyn is baseball. Her new friends see to it that Bandit joins a baseball team as right fielder. At bat, she hits a spectacular home run, and that earns her even more friends. Meanwhile, the Brooklyn Dodgers are winning the World Series, and Dodger star Jackie Robinson comes to visit her school. Shirley Temple Wong is chosen to give him the key to the school.

Bette learned a lot about prejudice and being accepted when she was a girl in Brooklyn. Her book tells how it feels to be a stranger in a new land. It can hurt and be hard. But life is a lot like baseball. Bette writes that every player on a baseball team must stand alone at bat. Each player can make a difference and can make it a new ball game even if the team is far behind. Believing these things helped Bette (and Bandit) succeed in the United States.

 2   What are you thinking about now?

Bette did not write this book about Shirley Temple Wong until long after her parents had brought her to Brooklyn. The communists took over in China, and Bette's parents decided not to go back there. They did not see Sansan for a long time.

Bette and her parents moved to New Jersey, and Bette went to high school there and then to college in Boston. After graduating from college, she met and married a man named Winston Lord. Not long after that, Bette Bao Lord was reunited with Sansan. That is when she decided to become a writer.

Her first book told of Sansan's hard life in China. It was called *Eighth Moon* and was a big success. Then Bette spent six years writing a book about five generations of one family. It was called *Spring Moon*.

Winston Lord was an American diplomat, so Bette Bao Lord returned to China with him several times. He represented the United States when he was there. Bette gave him advice and translated for him. By that time, she had raised her own family and had written several very successful books, including the one about Shirley Temple Wong.

Today, Bette Bao Lord is a well-known author. All of her books have been translated into many languages and are read by people all around the world.

 3 What are you thinking about now?

Darken the circle before the correct answer.

6. **The name of the book based on Bette's life in Brooklyn is called _____.**
   Ⓐ *Spring Moon*
   Ⓑ *In the Year of the Boar and Jackie Robinson*
   Ⓒ *Eighth Moon*
   Ⓓ *How to Play Right Field*

7. **The name of Bette's sister is _____.**
   Ⓐ Sansan
   Ⓑ Shirley
   Ⓒ Bandit
   Ⓓ Jackie

8. **Bandit is chosen to give Jackie Robinson the key to the school because _____.**
   Ⓐ he is Chinese
   Ⓑ she wrote a book about him
   Ⓒ it is the year of the boar
   Ⓓ she loves baseball so much

9. **Both young Bette and Shirley Temple Wong sometimes felt _____.**
   Ⓐ they could not make a big difference
   Ⓑ different and left out
   Ⓒ powerful and angry
   Ⓓ it was time to get out of school

Write your answer on the lines below.

10. **How does Bandit win new friends in Brooklyn? Tell at least two things that she does.**

_____

_____

_____

_____

Why is the family on the basement steps?

Emily thought it was like going through the "Scare Palace" at the local amusement park. The lightning flashing outside streaked into the little windows at the top of the basement walls. The electricity had been knocked out a half hour before, and the lightning bolts were coming every few seconds.

Emily got instant glimpses of the washer and dryer at the other end of the room and of the shelves of supplies and paint along the wall. It was like trying to watch a flickering TV when you had lost all but a shred of the signal. She could see split seconds of her mother's face. It looked pale and blank. Her mother was sitting on the bottom step, looking up at her father and at Emily and her brothers, Josh and Sanders.

"She knows I can see her," Emily thought. "She is trying not to show any emotion." The thunder that followed each stroke of lightning rumbled into the next one. Emily was glad she couldn't see what was going on outside. The rumble that followed the loud crack after each bolt was caught up in the rumble made by the next one. It turned Emily's ears into an echoing tunnel of terrible sound.

 1   What are you thinking about now?

"This is exciting!" Josh whispered, his voice rasping like the invaders in the space movie they had watched the week before. Poor Sanders, the youngest in the family, shuddered. He was seated on the step just below Emily. She could see that he had his chin resting on his knees.

"Knock it off, Josh!" Emily said, almost swallowing her words.

There was a particularly loud crack outside. "Oh, neat!" Josh said.

"Stop it," Father said, calmly and coolly.

Quiet gripped the stairway instantly as though someone had hit "Off" on the TV remote.

"It's quieting down out there," Mother said.

"It always gets quiet before a tornado hits," Josh said.

"Cut it out, Josh," Sanders mumbled.

"Listen!" Josh said. "It will sound like a loud train when it goes by."

"If . . . " Father said. Emily couldn't see him now, but she was sure he was looking up at the rafters in the stairwell. It was the safest place for them to be if a tornado did hit in their neighborhood, he had decided.

It became as quiet as late night camping out by the lake. They were all listening for the terrible train. Every second stretched time like a rubber band. Emily almost wished it would get there and end the long wait. It was making her very nervous. Then she noticed. She wasn't the only one. Sitting beside her, Josh began to tremble all over.

"He's afraid!" Emily thought. "He's more afraid than I am. He is just trying to cover it up." She couldn't decide if that was a comfort or not. In a way, it frightened her more than ever to realize Josh was afraid, too. On the other hand, feeling less afraid than Josh made her feel strong.

 2 What are you thinking about now?

Finally, Father said, "It's over. The storm is over." He was standing up, Emily knew, because his voice was coming from above her head. "Mom and I will go up first and light some candles."

But there was no holding back the children. They scrambled up the stairs. As soon as there was candlelight, Emily and Sanders began looking and calling for Fluff. Just as the lights came back on, Sanders came in the family room carrying the kitten in his arms. She was hiding her head, tucked down into Sander's hug. She looked like a little white, furry pillow.

"She was hiding in one of the closets," Sanders said.

"I'm glad she's safe," Father said. "And we're all together again."

 3   What are you thinking about now?

Darken the circle before the correct answer.

11. The family is huddled on the steps because _____.
    - Ⓐ they are being punished
    - Ⓑ a tornado has blown the house away
    - Ⓒ there is a very bad storm outside
    - Ⓓ invaders from space have landed

12. Why does Emily see parts of the basement for split seconds?
    - Ⓐ The lights are coming on and going off again.
    - Ⓑ Lightning is flashing through the windows.
    - Ⓒ She is trying to keep her eyes closed.
    - Ⓓ Sanders keeps standing up and blocking her view.

13. Why does Emily decide that Josh is afraid?
    - Ⓐ He keeps trying to be funny.
    - Ⓑ He isn't talking at all.
    - Ⓒ He keeps turning on the lights.
    - Ⓓ He trembles beside her.

14. Father is acting very _____.
    - Ⓐ frightened
    - Ⓑ foolish
    - Ⓒ strange
    - Ⓓ cautious

Write your answer on the lines below.

15. What do you think this sentence means: "Every second stretched time like a rubber band"?

_____

_____

_____

_____

_____

Acknowledgments

Grateful acknowledgment is made to the following authors and publishers for the use of copyrighted materials. Every effort has been made to obtain permission to use previously published material. Any errors or omissions are unintentional.

All for the Better: A Story of El Barrio by Nicholasa Mohr. Chapter 3, "People Are Hungry." Copyright © 1993 by Dialogue Systems, Inc.

"Cheetahs Are Fastest" by Jack Myers. Copyright © 1998 by Highlights for Children, Inc., Columbus, Ohio. Reprinted by permission of Highlights for Children, Inc.

"Giant Pandas" by John Bonnett Wexo. Copyright © 1998 Wildlife Education, Ltd. Reprinted by permission of Wildlife Education, Ltd.

Hoops by Robert Burleigh. Text copyright © 1997 by Robert Burleigh, illustration copyright © 1997 by Stephen T. Johnson. Reprinted by permission of Harcourt Inc.

July Is a Mad Mosquito by J. Patrick Lewis. Reprinted with the permission of Atheneum Books for Young Readers, an imprint of Simon & Schuster Children's Publishing Division, from JULY IS A MAD MOSQUITO by J. Patrick Lewis. Text copyright © 1994 J. Patrick Lewis.

"The Loch Ness Monster" by Brian Innes. From *Water Monsters* by Brian Innes. Copyright © 1999 by Steck-Vaughn Company.

"Shelly and the Great Purple Hairstreak" by Debbie A. Taylor. Reprinted, with permission, from *New Moon®: The Magazine for Girls and Their Dreams.* Copyright New Moon Publishing, Duluth, Minnesota.

"Skyskater" by T. C. Roth. Copyright © 1995 by Highlights for Children, Inc., Columbus, Ohio. Reprinted by permission of Highlights for Children, Inc.

"Stars in His Eyes" by Jack Rightmyer. Copyright © 1997 by Highlights for Children, Inc., Columbus, Ohio. Reprinted by permission of Highlights for Children, Inc.

Illustration Credits

Cindy Salans Rosenheim, pp. 4, 34, 76; Rudy Gutierrez, pp. 24, 28, 31; Kathleen O'Malley, cover, pp. 44–50; Richard Orr, p. 55; Walter Stuart, p. 57; Cheryl Kirk Noll, pp. 67, 69, 71, 72, 74; Dona Turner, cover, pp. 78–86; Marilee Heyer, cover, pp. 88–89, 90, 92, 94; Stephen T. Johnson, cover, pp. 96–112.

Photography Credits

Cover Sam Dudgeon; p. 5 Rick Williams; p. 7 © Gregory G. Dimijian/Photo Researchers Inc.; p. 9 Courtesy Eric B. Wheeldon, Ph.D.; p. 13 (inset) © Tony Korody/Sygma; pp. 13 (background), 14, 15 © PhotoDisc; p. 17 Sojourner®, Mars Rover® and spacecraft design and images © copyright 1996-97, California Institute of Technology. All rights reserved. Further reproduction prohibited; p. 18 © Buzzelli/O'Brien/Tom Stack & Associates; pp. 21, 22 CORBIS/Bettmann; p. 26 CORBIS; p. 35 Rick Williams; p. 36 © Ken Ross/Liaison International; p. 38 Popperfoto/Archive Photos; pp. 40, 42 © G. De Keerle/Gamma Liaison; p. 52 © Tim Davis/Photo Researchers, Inc.; pp. 53, 55 (background) © Will & Deni McIntyre/Photo Researchers, Inc.; p. 56 (l) © Tom McHugh/Photo Researchers, Inc.; p. 56 (r) © Tim Davis/Photo Researchers, Inc.; p. 57 (background) © Will & Deni McIntyre/Photo Researchers, Inc.; p. 58 © Tom & Pat Leeson/Photo Researchers, Inc.; p. 59 © Will & Deni McIntyre/Photo Researchers, Inc.; p. 60 © Sidney Bahri/Photo Researchers; pp. 62, 65 Courtesy Philip Gonzalez; p. 77 Rick Williams; p. 119 © Mario Suriani/AP/Wide World Photos; p. 120 Photo File/Archive Photos.